Twisting Toward the Light

BARBARA ANN PARKER

Cover Design: Hannah Purbaugh
Cover Painting: Stephanie Oka
Book Interior Design: Natalia Junqueira

For all the wildflowers and weeds

Acknowledgments

Sincere appreciation to the following publications and organizations that previously published my poetry.

Westmoreland Arts and Heritage Festival
Honorable Mention for the poems, "2:00 AM" and "Broken"

Backbone Mountain Review
Publication of the poems, "Swallowing the Sea" and "Pink Sky Morning"

The Loyalhanna Review
Publication of the poems, "India" and "It's Only Make Believe"

From the Depths
Publication of a poem, "Wildflowers and Weeds"

Muddy River Poetry Review
Publication of a poem, "A History Channel Kind of Love"

Red River Review
Publication of a poem, "Last Call for Fireflies"

Red Poppy Review
Publication of a poem, "Words Matter"

Menopause Press
Publication of a poem, "Dwelling in the Tents of the Wicked"

Central Cambria High School Writing Festival
Adult Specialty Writing Contest
First Place Award for the poem, "Morning Mist"

Pennwriters Poetry Contest
Third Place Award for the poem, "If I Wrote Love Poems…"

Contents

Part I - I Am 1
    My Song 2
    It's Only Make-Believe 3
    Broken 4
    In the Hour of my Father's Death 5
    Dear Nancy Lee, ... 6
    2:00 Am 7

Part II - Here in the Mountains 8
    Pink Sky Morning 10
    Last Call for Fireflies 11
    Message in a Bottle 12
    Homecoming 13
    Morning Mist 14
    Becoming a Nun 15

Part III - Angels 17
    Angels on a Cigarette Break 18
    Women in White 19
    Everyone's Happy These Days 20
    What Poems Will You Write Now? 22
    Words Matter 23
    Angels 24

Part IV - Love like That 26
Dwelling in the Tents of the Wicked............................. 28
Swallowing the Sea.. 30
A Glimpse of Heaven 31
A History Channel Kind of Love.................................. 32
If I Wrote Love Poems... 33
India 34

Part V - Twisting toward the Light 37
I Don't Know Why You Don't Love Poetry. 38
Blue Cake 40
Wildflowers and Weeds 41
Tupperware People 42
In Flight.. 43
Who Raised You? 44

PART 1
I Am

My Song

(Inspired by *Song of Myself* by Walt Whitman)

My song is a funeral march played backwards on a turntable.
No melody here.
The record is broken.
I am out of tune, off-key,
a seashell with no ocean sound.
I am a Halloween costume turned inside out, normal outside, all the scary stuff inside.

It's Only Make-Believe

Every day, I put on my pretty dress and my happy face and go out into the world.

You see me, laughing,
acting smart,
pretending to be wise,
and you think I've got my act together.

But inside I'm a withering hag,
Snow White's evil stepmother.
Every day, I eat the pretty, red apple,
swallowing the poison, trying to kill the darkness inside.

But every day, it lives.
It lives.
And I put on my pretty dress and my happy face and go out into the world.

Broken

I hold his poems in the palm of my hand.
He uses words of pain and love in equal measure,
trauma between the lines, love in the curve of the words.
Like looking in a Wonderland mirror, I see myself,
capable of creation and destruction,
bleeding and cutting,
broken,
yet capable of reflecting and holding light.

In the Hour of my Father's Death

Do not die a slow, painful death.
Do not die a sad, broken man.
Do not die in a hospital bed, miserably begging to come home.
Do not add one more drop of misery to a bottomless well of pain.
Do not, in your final hour, make me feel sorry for you.

Die like you lived:
your fist raised in defiance of God,
your middle finger raised in defiance of everyone else.

Die with your black heart filled with bitter hate.
Die with your rage like a shield raised to protect you as you go into
    the afterlife.
Die like you lived.

If you are not going to say the things you need to say,
if you are not going to say the things I so desperately need to hear.

Damn you to hell.
Die like you lived.

Dear Nancy Lee,

Shivering with my ass wrapped in an oversized paper towel, I have been waiting forty-five minutes.
There is a lovely painting of daises on the wall.
Signed by Nancy Lee
Who is Nancy Lee to me?
Was Nancy Lee here waiting like this?
Why is there a red button on the wall?
Is it a panic button?
"Lie down with your knees apart," the doctor commands.
Don't panic, Nancy Lee.
"Just try to relax," the nurse adds.
The cold metal pries me open.
Nancy Lee, be a dear and push the red button for me.
Nancy Lee! Push the button!
Nancy Lee, Push the damn button!
"There, that wasn't so bad, was it?" the doctor says.

2:00 Am

The angel of death has got me,
holding my throat with his skeleton hands,
and I can't breathe,
and every rotten, miserable thing I've ever done is coming back to me,
and I'm prayin',
prayin' to die.
Because I know,
like the goddamn ghost of Christmas future,
he's going to point his bony finger
into the darkness,
and there will be nothing there,
at least nothing I can see at 2:00 AM

PART II
Here in the Mountains

Pink Sky Morning

Pink sky morning
sailor's warning
calling out to me here in the mountains where the leaves are turning
    from green to gold to brown

I want to run shouting to every broken-down home, every rusted
    trailer, every disillusioned soul in every claustrophobic town.

I want to tell them that they're fading away inch-by-inch, day-by-day.
I want to tell them they have to go.
They cannot stay.
They need to feel, to reach, to dream.
I want to tell them,
The end is closer than it seems.

I want to tell them the sky is falling.
The angel of death is calling.
But they wouldn't believe.
They wouldn't hear.
not when everything is so calm
so ordinary
so rose colored.

Last Call for Fireflies

At the edge of the field, their lights blink
as they call for a mate.
But these are the unlucky fireflies.
Late in August,
the mating season is ending,
still they blink,
hopefully,
though their chances grow dimmer and dimmer
in the lavender dusk.

Message in a Bottle

What is my message?
Do I have anything to say in this twenty-ounce plastic space?
released in the water, floating toward the sea

And who will receive this message on the other side of the world?
Their bare feet licked by the ocean
my wet bottle dripping in their hands
Will they open it or toss it carelessly back to me?
back across the sea

And, if they opened it, would they find a blank white piece of paper?
Or maybe just the words,
I'm sorry.
Or I'm lonely
Would you be my friend across the sea?
And would you write a letter back to me?
And would it reach me?
Here in the mountains where there is no sea.

And then I realize there is no message in my bottle except…

I'm sorry.
I have no message.
I just wanted to reach out.

Homecoming

I have been away too long.
The prodigal daughter home from the wilderness,
I am beat down, road weary, and bone tired.

I see the mountains,
winter-white in the fading afternoon light,
tree branches glazed with ice.

My heart beats faster; my eyes fill with tears.

I see the courthouse,
its green dome reaching toward the winter sky,
the center of town, unchanging stone.

I watch snow move in tiny white swirls.
Something in me eases, lets go.
I am home.

Morning Mist

Fog wraps itself around the mountains, hiding the sun.
On the highway, a bus of gospel singers glides by,
salvation in a blue and silver tin can.
I think of the gospel singers,
mouths open,
thirsting for the Lord's glory.
It starts to rain, softly,
falling on my lips, on the sleeve of my black coat.
But it is only a mist,
not enough to quench my thirst,
not enough to baptize me.

Becoming a Nun

At the Catholic college with bright white statues of nuns,
staring down at us,
we comment,
no one wants to be a nun anymore.
My friend jokes, "You need a new career."
I laugh. "That would be a big win for God."

But then I think about it.

I'd have to study scripture,
know the doctrine,
follow the rules,
bow before God.

But what if I could?
What if I could give it all to God?
Be simple.
Be humble.
What if I could let go?

What if I could be lifted by the hands of saints to see the face of God?

What would it feel like bathing in the light?

What would it feel like?
Freeing
Powerful
Earth shattering
A spiritual orgasm

What would it feel like to believe?

PART III
Angels

Angels on a Cigarette Break

When someone dies young, we offer condolences.
"Things happen for a reason."
"God has a plan."
"He is with the angels now."

Every rotten, miserable jerk gets to live to a ripe, old age,
spreading their wickedness like a dark, festering plague.
Their angels never lose sight of them.

But where were your angels?
Did they step out for a cigarette?
Why did they look away?
Why did they let you fall?

Women in White

Here for their children's graduation,
where someone else will take the photos, and they will take the glory,
the women in white sit on the patio, a glass of wine in their hands,
the perfect white tips of their French manicures,
glistening in the sun.

Their hair is bleached blonde. Some of them wear their mother's pearls,
a generational chain that will not break and will not stain.
Some wear gold jewelry against their spray-tanned skin.
And their husbands, all shiny shoes and gelled hair, are nothing,
in comparison to these crisp ladies as white as laundry on the clothesline.

And as they rise from their seats, leaving behind the stain of lipstick
    and the floral scent of expensive perfume, they are both the white
    flags of surrender and the sails of the ship.

Everyone's Happy These Days

Why do I always screw things up?
Why do I always ruin things?
Why do things have to be the way they are?
I thought I could get over you, but I tried, and I can't.
Why can't you see how I feel?
I still love you for all the same reasons.
And I would give anything to have you hold me one last time.

I found this note inside a copy of *Brave New World*
that I bought at the Salvation Army Thrift Store,
the gray 49¢ tag still on the cover.
On the other side of the note,
stars, hearts, and smiley faces were doodled around Nichole's name.

I think of Nichole.
What did she screw up?
What are all the same reasons?
Who does she still love?

The note is dated 9-25-01.
Just after 9/11.
In those hours, days, and weeks of uncertainty
when everything was more intense, more real
Is this how Nichole felt about her lost love?
more real
more intense

I read the book.
Huxley's *Brave New World* discourages romantic attachments.
Everything complicated and messy like birth, death, and love is
    destroyed by the need for order and Soma pills.
"Everyone's happy these days," they chant mechanically.
Only the savages grow old, give birth, love.

I think of Nichole.
Did she find her lost love?
Has she found some new savage love?
Is she happy these days?

What Poems Will You Write Now?

You post pictures of Afghanistan, and I taste dust in my mouth.
You post pictures of you in fatigues, far from home, and I worry.
You are not my daughter or my sister, but I worry just the same.

I think of a poem you wrote about driving around at night after having
    your heart broken.
It is a poem of the young, the innocent, and I wonder,
What poems will you write now?

Words Matter

(For F. Scott and Zelda)

Words Matter
Her tongue so sharp, each kiss draws blood
My tongue so forked; every kiss poisons.

She is in the other room writing her own brand of poetry,
stringing together words like a lovely pearl necklace
that chokes.

I'm standing by the window, awaiting the executioner's bullet,
smoking my last cigarette,
searching for my last words.

Did we meet in May or June?
Was she wearing blue or violet?
Did I love her too much,
not enough,
not at all?

I listen to the scratch of her black pen against the cold, white page,
a death knell in the silence.

Angels

The hot, summer night air shines on your skin as you dance,
glorious grace.
Your body shimmers and sways like metallic smoke.
You throw your arms in the air as if praising an unseen God,
and for a moment, I believe in angels.

PART IV
Love like That

Dwelling in the Tents of the Wicked

I like the way curse words slither across my forked tongue and strike
    out of my mouth with venomous fire.
I like all the rotten, festering, twisted thoughts living in my dirty mind.

You think I'm Lilith rejecting Adam and defying God.
You think I'm Eve taking a bite out of the apple and a bite out of Adam.
You think I'm Satan, slimy and cold, wrapped around a sinner's tree.

But the truth is…
I'm not nearly as wicked as you need me to be.

Close your eyes against my immoral stare.
See no evil
Cover your ears against my wanton words
Hear no evil
Shield your untouched, pure heart against my corrupting words.
Speak no evil

Truth is…
I'm not seeking salvation, and you spend a lot of time trying to save me.

You like to click your tongue and wag your finger in judgment.
It makes you feel so good about your untainted soul.
So damn holy
So damn righteous
So damn clean

But I think you like the way I look at you.
You want my black heart, my sinner's body, and my corrupt mind.
You covet my kind of freedom,
my kind of fire.

You like to think I'm coming for you
to infect you
to corrupt you
to mold you into me.

Truth is…
I'm not really thinking of you, and you spend a lot of time thinking
    of me.

Swallowing the Sea

Like Calypso, nymph of the sea, I want to keep you,
treasure you with an intimate kiss,
taste your salt on my tongue,
Make you a god.

A Glimpse of Heaven

In the vastness of space,
there are a billion stars glowing,
a trillion fragments of space rock, slivers of asteroids, and specks of comets
floating in the shadows.
We, two traces of space dust, meet in infinite darkness.

You think our meeting is a cosmic disaster,
that we will burn up in each other's atmospheres,
collide into each other, exploding,
plummet to the earth, shattering and spreading debris.

I think it is nothing short of astronomical, nothing short of astrological
    that we converge at all.
And, if I am wrong, it is nothing but a flicker in the vastness of space
    and time,
nothing
but for a moment we were not alone in the darkness.

A History Channel Kind of Love

Ancient Mayans, Ancient Chinese, and modern scientists all agree.
2012
Winter Solstice
The sun, the moon, the earth, and the Milky Way all in a perfect line
The earth turns upside down.
North is South. South is North.
Earthquakes
Floods
Disaster
The end of the world

Will you love me as if it were true?
As if there was not enough time to analyze every thought, every feeling,
    every action

Will you?
Will you love me as if there were no happily ever after?
Because there will be no ever after.

Will you stand with me in the moment?
In the place with no beginning and no end
In the place of now

Will you?
Will you love me as if the History Channel was right?

If I Wrote Love Poems...

Lightning bolts chase me across the darkness.
Thunder follows me with the sound of a beating heart.
Mars is there in the stormy August sky, fiery and red.
Cupid's arrows cannot penetrate a hardened heart like mine, so he
    sends down Mars, the god of war, the god of lightning and thunder.

I seek refuge under the florescent lights of an open all night grocery
    store.
Like Odysseus on his journey, I am lost and lonely.
I wander the aisles in search of the food that will make it better,
the person who will make it less lonely.

And there you are
like Penelope, waiting,
among the sweet young peas and the fresh new corn.
And I am happy to see you.

India

When my friend speaks of love, he speaks of India.

He speaks of food and drinks,
spicy air.

He speaks of crazy passion,
heat upon her skin.

He speaks of romantic movies,
colorful tapestries.

He speaks of the spark of new love
under the night sky.

When my friend speaks of love, he speaks of India.
And I think, I'd like to love like that.

PART V
Twisting toward the Light

I Don't Know Why You Don't Love Poetry.

I don't know why you don't love poetry.
the way it snaps, pops, and hisses like a fire.
the way it shoots like lightning from the top of your head to the soles of your feet
the way it opens you up and fills you like warm chocolate on your tongue
the way it sways you gently like the summer wind brushing over green blades of grass

Oh, I wish you could hear Beat poets
the way their voices rise up and float back down
the way they hold a word until the room vibrates
the way they move their bodies like they're being rocked by the hand of God

I don't know why you don't love poetry.

I bet you think it is all meter and rhyme.
Yes, that's poetry but not all of it.
No, no poetry is everywhere.

It's at a winter festival under a full moon on a hazy, January night.

It's in the little kid who leans forward on his toes and rocks back on his heels as he stands in line waiting for the salty-sweet taste of kettle corn.

It's in the sound that the corn makes inside the large silver kettle as it is heated by a bright blue flame.
Pop! Pop! Pop!

It's in the West Virginian man's voice as he says, "I know there was pain in their hearts. I wasn't kin to none of those miners. But they were my brothers just like you're my brother, and you're my brother. In Christ."

The way he holds the word, pain until you feel it in your chest. The way he repeats the word brother until you want to follow him to the river and be baptized.

I don't know why you don't love poetry.

Blue Cake

At the state park, encircled by green trees, humidity clings to my skin
    and steals my breath.
The lake water is not shockingly cold but perfectly cool.
I float. The water fills my ears, shutting off sound.
There is nothing but me, the water, the sun, and the bluest of blue skies.
Later, when the sun bends to kiss the treetops, we eat cake, soft,
    sweet, and dyed to match the blue summer sky.

Wildflowers and Weeds

(for my friends)

Wildflowers and Weeds
bloom
in rocky soil
in mud
among trash.

Wildflowers and Weeds
huddle together,
sharing dirt,
basking in the sun,
enduring the wind.

Wildflowers and Weeds
get tangled together
and are made more beautiful
by the company they keep.

Tupperware People

My grandmother used to say that there's someone for everyone;
    every pot has a lid.
But Grandma never mentioned Tupperware.

After time and heat and pressure, the lids don't fit.
And the lids keep getting lost.
And everything gets stained.

Grandma never told me about Tupperware people.

Tough and resilient, Tupperware people do not need a lid.
They are not pots.
They are not made that way.

In Flight

When the wings of a blue Morpho butterfly are closed, they are brown, so they can blend in with the Earth, hiding from danger.

I kept myself closed, trying to hide, trying to blend in, so I would be safe.

And I stayed closed for so long; I forgot how to be beautiful, how to be loved.

I forgot how to fly.

When a blue Morpho butterfly opens its wings, they appear to be a brilliant blue. Except they're not blue.
Their wings have iridescent, reflective scales, so they only appear to be blue.

When I opened my wings wide, I blinded everyone with bright colors, noise,
and the bigness of me.

But that wasn't me either; it was everything I thought I should be,
so I could be heard,
so I could be seen.

But no matter how big, how bright.
I still couldn't fly.

And then I realized it didn't matter what they
 saw; it mattered what I felt, what I knew.

I could be loved even when I was closed and afraid.

I could be seen in my own light.

I could be me in flight.

Who Raised You?

Once I said, "Women are raised to be nice, quiet, obedient."

Someone responded, "Who raised you?"

And I laughed.

But I had no answer.

Who raised me?

People tried to train, mold, and construct me.

Few people elevated or lifted me.

Who raised you?

Once, a little sapling appeared from under the coal mining house where I grew up. The sapling twisted and bent, trying to reach the sunlight.

We moved that tree to the backyard, and it grew.

Years after I was gone, years after the house was gone, the tree was still there, still twisted.

Who raised you?

No one

I just grew wild and twisting toward the light.

www.ingramcontent.com/pod-product-compliance
Lightning Source LLC
Chambersburg PA
CBHW050226100526
44585CB00017BA/2101